An Abbreviated Field Guide: Waterfowl of Illinois

by

Stephen P. Havera

Steve Havera
19 October 1999

Illinois Natural History Survey • Champaign
August 1999

Manual 7

Copyright ©1999 by the Illinois Natural History Survey
David L. Thomas, Chief

A Division of the Illinois Department of Natural Resources
Brent Manning, Director

Printed by authority of the State of Illinois
George Ryan, Governor
SR900360—3M—8—99
ISBN 1-882932-02-1

Library of Congress Card Catalog Number: 99-71744
An Abbreviated Field Guide: Waterfowl of Illinois

Edited by Audrey S. Hodgins
Designed by Randee Bowlin, Technica
Illustrated by Michelle M. Georgi
Cover designed by Steven Bowlin, Technica
Cover painting of Northern Pintails
    by Beverley C. Sanderson

Citation:
Havera, S.P. 1999. Waterfowl of Illinois: an abbreviated field guide.
Illinois Natural History Survey Manual 7. viii + 72 pp.

This publication is printed with soy ink on recycled and recyclable
paper.

This guide is dedicated to
waterfowl and their habitat resources in Illinois.

Contents

Acknowledgments ix

Introduction 1

One: Wetlands 5

Two: Habitat Programs Beneficial
to Wetlands and Waterbirds 7

Three: The Illinois Natural History Survey's
Aerial Inventories of Waterfowl 9

Four: Banding 11

Five: Some Important Natural Plant Foods
of Ducks in Illinois 13

Six: Some Important Animal Foods
of Ducks in Illinois 18

Seven: Waterfowl and Coots Common to Illinois 20

Dabbling Ducks
Mallard 22
American Black Duck 24
Northern Pintail 26
Blue-winged Teal 28
Green-winged Teal 30
American Wigeon 32
Gadwall 34
Northern Shoveler 36

Perching Ducks
Wood Duck 38

Diving Ducks
Lesser Scaup 40
Canvasback 42
Ring-necked Duck 44
Redhead 46
Ruddy Duck 48

Common Goldeneye 50
Common Merganser 52
Hooded Merganser 54
Coots
American Coot 55
Geese
Canada Goose 57
Lesser Snow Goose 60

Eight: Illinois Waterfowl Milestones 62

Nine: Observing Waterbirds 64

Suggested Reading 68

MICHELLE GEORGI

A field-feeding flock of Mallards, a common scene during fall and winter.

Acknowledgments

Information for this abbreviated field guide was primarily summarized from the companion volume *Waterfowl of Illinois: Status and Management*. Consequently those contributors acknowledged in the primary volume indirectly contributed to this field guide. Nevertheless, the efforts and support of my Natural History Survey colleagues Lynn L. Anderson, Michelle M. Georgi, Christopher S. Hine, Elizabeth C. Loebach, Katie E. Roat, and Aaron P. Yetter made this field guide possible. In addition, Patrick W. Brown, Glen C. Sanderson, and Timothy R. Van Deelen reviewed the manuscript, Audrey S. Hodgins edited the text and Tom Humburg provided us with many of the photos.

Introduction

Illinois lies in the heart of the Mississippi Flyway with the breeding grounds to the north and the wintering grounds to the south. The Illinois River bisects the northern two-thirds of the state, the Mississippi River flanks the western boundary of Illinois, and the Ohio River delineates its southeastern border. The prairies prevalent in east-central Illinois prior to European settlement were rich in wetlands. The renowned Winnebago Swamp, Kankakee Marsh, northeastern glacial marshes, and baldcypress-tupelo gum swamps in the southern tip of the state were remarkable wetlands that complemented the luxurious bottomlands of the river floodplains.

Because of the high quality and abundance of its wetlands, Illinois welcomed legions of nesting and migratory waterfowl and other waterbirds. A strong and colorful waterfowl tradition emerged in the Prairie State, particularly along the Illinois and Mississippi rivers. Private duck clubs were established in the late 1800s, some of which remain in operation today. Market hunters found abundant supplies of waterfowl that were shipped to restaurants throughout the eastern United States. Carvers of wooden decoys, such as Elliston, Graves, Perdew, and Walker, and the makers of duck calls, including Allen, Ditto, and Olt, embellished the Illinois waterfowl tradition. The first large-scale trapping of waterfowl for research in the United States took place near Browning on the Illinois River in 1922. Few other states have such a history and depth of waterfowl information.

Although its landscapes have changed dramatically in the past two centuries, Illinois still hosts significant numbers of waterfowl and other waterbirds, especially during fall and spring migrations, and will continue to do so. There is an indescribable lure about waterfowl that captures our interest, whether we are birdwatchers, conservationists, outdoor enthusiasts, or hunters. We want to know what kinds of waterfowl frequent our state, when, where, how many, what they eat, where they nest, and what we can do to enjoy or help them.

As a result of the intense as well as the casual interest of many, this abbreviated guide was produced to make available selected highlights from its companion volume, *Waterfowl of Illinois: Status and Management*, and is not an all-inclusive examination of the natural history aspects of those species of waterfowl frequenting Illinois.

Canada Geese resting on a frozen lake.

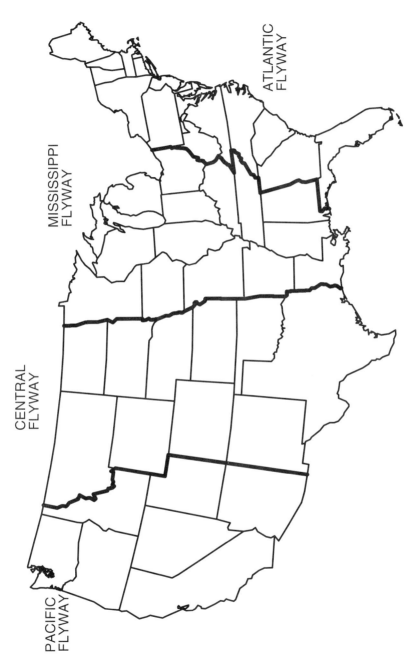

Figure 1. *The four flyways (Pacific, Central, Mississippi, and Atlantic) were established in 1947 by the United States Fish and Wildlife Service for the purpose of formulating management policies and goals as well as waterfowl hunting regulations in accordance with differences in migration corridors and wetlands throughout the country.*

Wetlands in the Illinois River valley floodplain.

ONE

Wetlands

Waterbird habitat includes wetlands, deepwater habitats, and areas with water levels manipulated for management.

Wetlands are areas where water saturation is the dominant factor that determines soil development and the plant and animal communities that live in the soil as well as on its surface. Wetlands are transitional lands between terrestrial and aquatic systems where the land is covered by shallow water or the water table is near or at the surface. Wetlands must have one or more of three characteristics:

1. the land supports, at least periodically, predominantly hydrophytic (water-loving) plants;

2. the substrate is composed of predominantly undrained hydric soils;

3. the substrate is nonsoil and saturated or covered by shallow water sometime during the growing season each year.

Wetlands include marshes, swamps, ponds, potholes, bogs, sloughs, wet meadows, mud flats, and river overflows. Deepwater habitats are permanently flooded lands that lie below the deepwater boundary of wetlands.

During Colonial America, wetlands comprised 221 million acres in the conterminous United States. By the mid-1970s, about 106 million acres remained in the contiguous 48 states. In Illinois, at least 8.2 million acres of wetlands existed prior to European settlement, covering approximately 23 percent of the state. A recent survey of wetlands in Illinois revealed nearly 918,000 acres of natural wetlands, only 2.6 percent of the state. Illinois has lost approximately 90 percent of its original wetlands and most of those that remain have been affected by sedimentation or other deleterious effects of human activity.

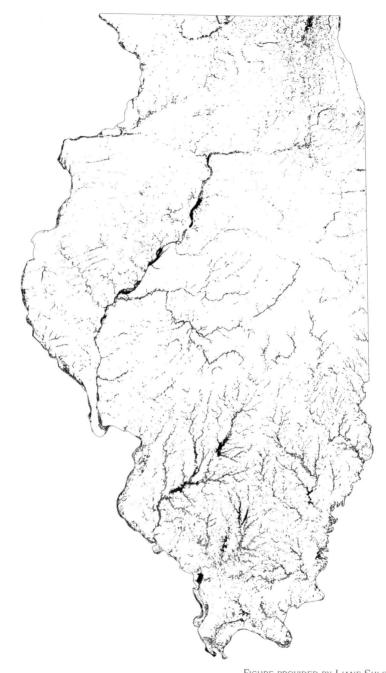

Figure 2. *The distribution of wetlands in Illinois,* 1980–1987.

TWO

Habitat Programs Beneficial to Wetlands and Waterbirds

One of the most heralded conservation programs is the **North American Waterfowl Management Plan**. This program stems from an agreement initiated in 1986 between the United States and Canada (Mexico joined in 1994) to implement a 15-year plan to ensure the survival of waterfowl populations and to enhance and protect high-quality wetland habitat in North America. In 1994, the plan called for the protection of over 11 million acres, the restoration of over 5 million acres, and the enhancement of almost 10 million acres.

Another important program is the **Conservation Reserve Program**. Administered by the U.S. Department of Agriculture, its primary purpose is to remove highly erodible land from production and to plant it to protective cover. Landowners are paid annual per acre rental payments for 10 years, or 15 years if trees are planted. In addition, they are reimbursed for one-half the cost of establishing permanent cover. Approximately 36 million acres were enrolled by 1995 (772,000 acres in Illinois).

The **Wetland Reserve Program** is a voluntary easement program designed to help landowners restore and protect 975,000 acres of wetlands now in agricultural use by the year 2000. Financial incentives are offered for landowners who grant 30-year or longer easements. Priority areas include farmed wetlands and former wetlands that had been converted to other uses. This program is the largest government wetland restoration undertaking in the nation's history and has the potential to contribute significantly to the restoration of aquatic ecosystems.

One organization in particular that has played an important role in wetland and waterfowl conservation is **Ducks Unlimited**. According to Ducks Unlimited, nearly 80 percent of its income goes directly towards waterfowl and wetlands conservation and almost 8 million acres of habitat have been conserved since 1937. Ducks Unlimited also plays an active role in the North American Waterfowl Management Plan. Ducks Unlimited has habitat projects in the United States, Canada, and Mexico.

The U.S. Fish and Wildlife Service's **Partners for Wildlife** program improves and protects fish and wildlife habitat, including wetlands, on private lands through alliances with the Service and other federal agencies, state and municipal agencies, nongovernment organizations, and individuals. The land is left in private ownership. Technical and financial assistance is provided to landowners who undertake projects in the Partners for Wildlife program. From 1987 to 1996, the program restored more than 360,000 acres of wetlands in the United States.

Since 1934, the **Migratory Bird Hunting and Conservation Stamp** has generated over $500 million and helped to preserve more than 4.4 million acres of migratory bird refuge and nesting habitat through the purchase of easements and fee titles. Approximately 98 percent of the revenue generated from the sale of these federal duck stamps is used to purchase migratory waterfowl habitat.

From 1975 to 1995, receipts from the sale of state **Migratory Waterfowl Stamps** in Illinois totaled $7.9 million. One-half of these funds are used for approved projects for protecting waterfowl and improving public waterfowl areas in the state; one-fourth of the proceeds go to nonprofit organizations for the development of water-fowl production areas in Canada or the United States; another fourth goes to nonprofit organizations for the development of waterfowl areas under the North American Waterfowl Management Plan in Canada or the United States. From 1975 to 1992, the Illinois Migratory Waterfowl Stamp Program acquired approximately 3,000 acres of wetlands and completed 15 habitat development projects in the state and partially or entirely financed 10 projects in Canada.

The **Pittman-Robertson Act** enacted in 1937 created the Federal Aid in Wildlife Restoration Program for allocation of funds to the states. Revenue is generated from excise taxes on the sale of sporting arms and ammunition, archery equipment, and handguns. States can use these funds for management, acquisition, or restoration of wildlife habitat and associated research. From 1937 to 1984, Illinois acquired 25,774 acres of habitat for migratory birds with funds provided by this act.

THREE

The Illinois Natural History Survey's Aerial Inventories of Waterfowl

The Illinois River valley from Spring Valley to Grafton and the Mississippi River valley from Alton to Moline have been periodically inventoried in the fall since 1948 by members of the Illinois Natural History Survey. Inventories during spring have been conducted

intermittently since 1955. Other areas throughout the state have been added over the years and flown for various periods (see map, page 10). From 1948 to 1970, weekly inventories were made by Frank C. Bellrose. From 1971 through 1989, they were

MICHELLE GEORGI

A concentration of waterfowl as it appears during an aerial inventory.

conducted by Robert D. Crompton, and from 1990 through the present, the inventories have been made by Michelle M. Georgi.

The purpose of the aerial inventories is not to acquire complete counts of the waterfowl numbers within the areas surveyed but to estimate the numbers of each species in order to provide an index of changes within and among years and to document the distribution of the species observed throughout the various wetlands in the inventory regions.

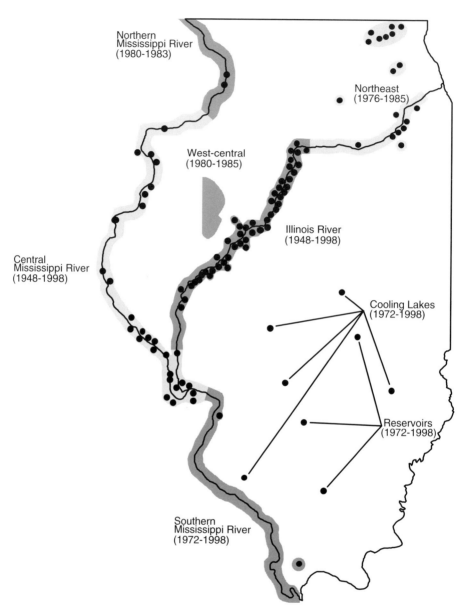

Figure 3. *Specific locations within and the general areas of the northern, central, and southern Mississippi River; the Illinois River; the northeast and west-central regions; and the selected cooling lakes and reservoirs in central and southern Illinois aerially inventoried for waterfowl by the Illinois Natural History Survey for various periods since 1948.*

FOUR

Banding

The banding of migratory waterfowl is one of the most important and powerful tools of research and management. The data recovered from bands are used to plot migration patterns and to identify geographic distributions of populations. When combined with harvest and population information, banding data provide insights into waterfowl production, survival, and harvest.

The U.S. Fish and Wildlife Service bands currently found on waterfowl carry variations of one of three inscriptions:

1. "AVISE BIRD BAND WRITE WASHINGTON DC USA" (avise meaning report);

2. "WRITE: BIRD BAND, U.S. FISH AND WILDLIFE SERVICE, LAUREL, MD 20708 USA";

3. "CALL 800–327–BAND OR WRITE: BIRD BAND, U.S. FISH AND WILDLIFE SERVICE, LAUREL, MD 20708, USA".

MICHELLE GEORGI

Three styles of U.S. Fish and Wildlife Service waterfowl bands.

It is important that waterfowl hunters inform the U.S. Fish and Wildlife Service of the following for all bands recovered: the band number, the date and location of recovery, the species, and the name and mailing address of the finder. The band may be kept, and a certificate with the biological history of the bird will be sent to the person reporting the band.

Banding studies provide important information. For example, a large difference may exist between the maximum age of a bird and its average life span. Male Mallards have been known to live from 18 to 29 years and females from 16 to 18; however, they normally live approximately 2 years. Females generally have a shorter life span because nesting makes them more susceptible to predation.

FIVE

Some Important Natural Plant Foods of Ducks in Illinois

STEPHEN HAVERA

American Wild Celery
(Eelgrass, Wild celery)
Vallisneria americana

Wild celery grows in quiet water in the northern half of the state and may occur at considerable depths beneath the water's surface. Ducks utilize the entire plant but are particularly fond of the winter buds and tubers. It is a favorite food of Canvasbacks, which have a similar scientific name of *Aythya valisineria*.

MICHELLE GEORGI

Common Arrowhead
(Duck Potato, Arrowleaf)
Sagittaria latifolia

Common arrowhead is found in swamps, sloughs, ponds, shorelines, shallow water, and mud. It is more common in the northern and central counties of Illinois. This plant is valued by ducks for its seeds and tubers.

Common Barnyard Grass
(Wild Millet, Common Millet)
Echinochloa crusgalli

Common barnyard grass is found on mud flats. It occurs occasionally throughout Illinois. This plant provides cover for ducks as well as seeds for food.

Common Hornwort
(Coontail)
Ceratophyllum demersum

Coontail grows best in stable or semistable waters that are fairly clear and protected from waves. It occurs commonly throughout Illinois. Ducks feed mostly on the leaves and stems.

Curltop Ladysthumb
(Nodding Smartweed)
Polygonum lapathifolium

Curltop ladysthumb is found on moist, disturbed soil and is common throughout Illinois. Waterfowl feed on its seeds.

MICHAEL JEFFORDS

Duckweed
Lemna spp.

Duckweeds float on the surface of water throughout the state. *Lemna* species are very sensitive to metals and other pollutants.

PHOTO COURTESY OF
U.S. ARMY CORPS OF ENGINEERS,
ST. PAUL DISTRICT

Fennelleaf Pondweed
(Sago Pondweed)
Potamogeton pectinatus

Fennelleaf pondweed grows best at depths of 2 to 4 feet in lakes with stable water throughout Illinois. This plant is an important food source for ducks because of the high palatability of its foliage, seeds, and tubers.

STEPHEN HAVERA

Flatsedges
(Nutgrass, Sedge)
Cyperus spp.

These plants grow on mud flats and mud banks of rivers and are found throughout Illinois. In some cases, ducks clip off the seed heads of the plant; in other cases, individual seeds are strained from the bottom ooze or the surface of the water. Canada Geese are more likely to eat the shoots of the plant.

Leafy Pondweed
(Pondweed)
Potamogeton foliosus

Leafy pondweed is found in ponds, lakes, rivers, and streams throughout the state. The seeds and foliage are consumed by several species of ducks.

STEPHEN HAVERA

Muskgrass
(Chara)
Chara spp.

Muskgrass is an algae with cylindrical, whorled branches. It is almost always found in mineral-rich water, such as strip-mined lakes, and often has incrustations of lime. The entire plant is a food source for ducks throughout Illinois.

PHOTO COURTESY OF U.S. ARMY CORPS OF ENGINEERS, ST. PAUL DISTRICT

PHOTO COURTESY OF
U.S. ARMY CORPS OF ENGINEERS,
ST. PAUL DISTRICT

Pennsylvania Smartweed
(Largeseed or Common
Smartweed)
Polygonum pensylvanicum

This plant grows on moist ground associated with wetlands. Three varieties are found in Illinois. Utilization of the seeds of this plant by ducks changes from year to year depending upon availability and accessibility.

STEPHEN HAVERA

Rice Cutgrass
(Sawgrass)
Leersia oryzoides

Rice cutgrass grows on moist soil and in shallow water. It occurs occasionally throughout Illinois and is a preferred food of many species of ducks. Ducks feed on its roots and seeds.

Some Important Animal Foods of Ducks in Illinois

DENISE STOECKEL

Burrowing Mayflies
Hexagenia spp.

Burrowing mayfly nymphs inhabit the muddy bottoms of shallow, fresh waters. They are an important food source of diving ducks, especially along the Mississippi River.

RON SORIN

Dragonfly Nymphs
Aeschnidae

These nymphs are common on submerged vegetation on the bottom of ponds, marshes, streams, and in shallow areas of lakes.

RICHARD SPARKS

Fingernail Clams

(Pillclam, Nutclam)

Musculium transversum
Sphaerium striatinum

Fingernail clams are found in sediment, mud, sand, and gravel in freshwater lakes and rivers, such as Pool 19 of the Mississippi River. They are a favorite food of diving ducks, particularly Lesser Scaups or bluebills.

MARLA ROSALES

Freshwater Snails

Gastropoda

These snails are found in almost every type of freshwater habitat, from the smallest ponds to the largest lakes and rivers. They colonize on submerged surfaces, mostly in water from a few inches to 6 feet deep.

MARLA ROSALES

Midge Larvae

(Blood Worm)
Chironomidae

Midge larvae are common on aquatic vegetation and in the bottom of bodies of fresh water.

SEVEN

Waterfowl and Coots Common to Illinois

Of the ten common species of dabbling ducks in North America, eight are particularly important to Illinois—the Mallard, American Black Duck, Northern Pintail, Blue-winged Teal, Green-winged Teal, American Wigeon, Gadwall, and Northern Shoveler. The feet of the dabbling ducks are placed near the middle of the body, and the hind toes lack the lobe of skin that is present in diving ducks. When taking flight, they spring directly upward from the water. While feeding, they often tip up and submerge their heads with their tails showing above the shallow water.

Although the Wood Duck resembles a dabbling duck in general appearance, it is placed in the category of perching ducks. These ducks have legs that are farther forward than those of dabbling ducks, sharp strong claws, well-developed hind toes, and broad wings. The Wood Duck is the only species of perching duck that inhabits North America above Mexico. It is the most abundant species of breeding ducks in Illinois.

The remaining ducks are all diving ducks that dive below the water surface to feed. They rarely nest in Illinois but are visitors during migration. There are three tribes—the bay, sea, and stiff-tailed ducks—which embrace twelve genera around the world. The bay ducks include the Lesser Scaup, Canvasback, Ring-necked Duck, and Redhead. The Common Goldeneye, mergansers, and Bufflehead are sea ducks and nest mostly in tree cavities. The mergansers have long, slender, serrated bills used to catch small fish and other aquatic prey. The Ruddy Duck, with tail feathers that are long, stout, and pointed, is a stiff-tailed duck. It feeds on organisms in sediments.

American Coots are often associated with waterfowl because they are the most aquatic members of the rail family. They move on open water like ducks and often feed with them. They are excellent swimmers and divers and feed mostly on aquatic plants.

Geese are distinct from other waterfowl because both sexes have similar plumage and both care for the young. They have one molt per year rather than two as is the case with ducks. Geese usually mate for life. They graze on a wide variety of plant foods.

Detailed nesting information is given only for those waterfowl species that commonly nest in Illinois.

Dabbling Ducks

Female and male   Tom Humburg

Mallard
(Greenhead [drake], Susie [hen])
Anas platyrhynchos

- During the breeding season the adult male Mallard has a pronounced green head with a white neck ring. Both male and female Mallards have a violet-blue speculum (a bright, iridescent patch on the wings) bordered by a white stripe at the front and back. The female has uniformly mottled brown body plumage with whitish tail feathers. Other prominent features of the female include a dark eye stripe and an orange and brown bill. The flight of the Mallard is not particularly rapid. They form loose groups when flying together.

- Mallards have recently begun to nest in all 102 counties of Illinois. They nest in a variety of situations near wetlands, ponds, streams, and lakes and in artificial nest structures. The female forms a nest bowl or scrape and lines it with grasses and down. Eggs vary from grayish buff to olive green, number from 6 to 10 with an average of about 9, and are 2.2 inches long by 1.2–1.6 inches wide. Incubation time is about 28 days.

- Food habit studies reveal that corn is the most important food for Mallards in Illinois. Like many other dabbling ducks, Mallards also prefer the seeds of other plants, such as rice cutgrass, Japanese millet, buckwheat, common barnyard grass, Pennsylvania smartweed, and curltop ladysthumb.

- The Mallard is the most vociferous of game ducks. Males utter a variety of soft, reedy notes. The females have a loud quack.

- The mean life span for adult male and female Mallards is approximately 2.1 and 1.6 years, respectively. The maximum known age for a wild banded Mallard is 29 years.

- The Mallard is the most highly prized duck by hunters in Illinois. It ranked first in number of ducks harvested in Illinois from 1991 to 1995 with a yearly average of 123,000. The Mallard also ranked first in the number of ducks harvested from 1991 to 1995 in the Mississippi Flyway with an average of more than 1.5 million taken each year. The highest, or peak, number of Mallards recorded during the aerial inventories each fall in the Illinois River and central Mississippi River regions showed a general decline from 1948 to 1996.

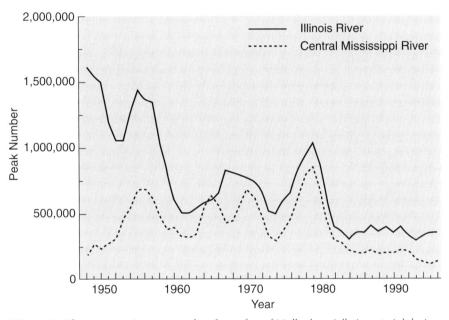

Figure 4. *Three-year moving average of peak numbers of Mallards aerially inventoried during fall in the Illinois River and the central Mississippi River regions, 1948–1996. A three-year moving average is the average of the peak number for a specific year and the two previous years and it is used to minimize annual fluctuations and to emphasize long-term trends.*

- Average Date of the Peak Fall Migration by Aerial Inventory Region (see map, page 10)

Illinois River Region	17–23 Nov.
Central Mississippi River Region	24–30 Nov.
Northeast Region	24 Nov.–7 Dec.
Southern Mississippi River Region	8–21 Dec.
Reservoirs and Cooling Lakes in Central and Southern Illinois	24 Nov.–7 Dec.

GEORGE ARTHUR

American Black Duck
(Black Mallard, Red Legs)
Anas rubripes

- American Black Ducks are
  similar to the female Mallard
  in plumage. Both sexes have a
  purplish speculum bordered
  with black. The head and neck
  are somewhat lighter in color
  than the body. The bill of
  an adult male is olive to bright
  yellow; that of the female is olive-green with black mottling. In
  flight, the white underneath the wings is visible. This duck
  resembles the Mallard in body conformation, size, and flight
  characteristics. The American Black Duck appears black only at
  a distance and was formerly known as the "dusky duck." It is
  considered the wariest of all ducks.

- American Black Ducks rarely nest in Illinois.

- The American Black Duck utters a call similar to that of
  the Mallard.

- The average life span for adult male and female American Black
  Ducks is 2.2 and 1.3 years, respectively. The maximum known age
  for a wild banded American Black Duck is 26 years.

- American Black Ducks are often seen in the company of
  Mallards, but the peak number of American Black Ducks
  represents only a small percentage of the number of Mallards
  that pass through Illinois during fall.

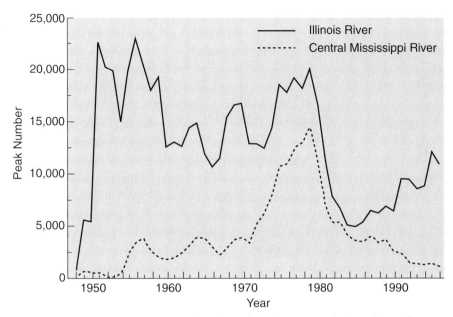

Figure 5. *Three-year moving average of peak numbers of American Black Ducks aerially inventoried during fall in the Illinois River and the central Mississippi River regions, 1948–1996.*

- Average Date of the Peak Fall Migration by Aerial Inventory Region (see map, page 10)

Illinois River Region	24–30 Nov.
Central Mississippi River Region	1–7 Dec.
Northeast Region	24 Nov.–7 Dec.
Southern Mississippi River Region	8–21 Dec.
Reservoirs and Cooling Lakes in Central and Southern Illinois	24 Nov.–7 Dec.

Male   TOM HUMBURG

Female   MICHELLE GEORGI

Northern Pintail
(Sprig, Sprigtail)
Anas acuta

- The male Northern Pintail in breeding plumage has a brown head with a white streak extending down the sides of the neck to the breast and belly. In flight, the male has a visible green speculum with a white trailing edge. The female has mottled brown body plumage with a lighter brown head and breast. The speculum of the female Northern Pintail is brown with white on the trailing edge. Both male and female have a blue-gray bill. The body of a Northern Pintail is long and slender, and its tail is longer than that of most species. These slim, graceful birds, known as greyhounds of the air, are fast fliers that often zigzag down from great heights before leveling off to land.

- Historically, Northern Pintails were reported to nest sparingly in northeastern Illinois. Recently, they have been found nesting in nine counties (Cass, Cook, Ford, Grundy, Lake, McHenry, Mason, Shelby, Whiteside) in Illinois.

- Food habit studies reveal that the three most important food items for Northern Pintails in Illinois are corn, brittle naiad, and Pennsylvania smartweed.

- The elegant males have a short fluttering whistle; the females have a harsh quack.

- The average life span for adult male and female Northern Pintails is 3.0 and 2.0 years, respectively. The maximum known age for a wild banded Northern Pintail is 26 years.

- Moderate numbers of Northern Pintails occur in the Illinois and central Mississippi river regions.

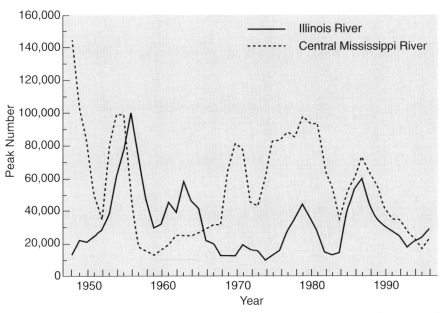

Figure 6. *Three-year moving average of peak numbers of Northern Pintails aerially inventoried during fall in the Illinois River and the central Mississippi River regions, 1948–1996.*

- **Average Date of the Peak Fall Migration by Aerial Inventory Region** (see map, page 10)

Illinois River Region	27 Oct.–2 Nov.
Central Mississippi River Region	27 Oct.–2 Nov., 10–16 Nov.
Northeast Region	13–26 Oct.
Southern Mississippi River Region	27 Oct.–9 Nov.
Reservoirs and Cooling Lakes in Central and Southern Illinois	27 Oct.–9 Nov.

A flock of sleek and graceful Northern Pintails in flight.
MICHELLE GEORGI

Male   TOM HUMBURG

Female   TOM HUMBURG

Blue-winged Teal
(Summer Teal)
Anas discors

- The breeding adult male Blue-winged Teal has a steel-blue head with a white crescent on each side of its face between the bill and the eye; however, these features are not present in their fall plumage. The female has a uniformly gray-brown body and a dark streak across the eye. Males have an iridescent green speculum whereas females have a dull non-iridescent green speculum. In flight, a chalky blue wing patch is visible; it may appear white under some lighting conditions. The small body size and the twisting, turning flight of the Blue-winged Teal give the illusion of great speed. Small, compact flocks often fly low over marshes and take the observer or hunter by surprise.

- Blue-winged Teals have been recently recorded as nesting in 66 counties and on 21 of 151 public sites in Illinois. They nest in grassy areas near water. The nest is made of grass and weeds. Eggs are a creamy tan and number from 6 to 15 with an average of about 10 per nest. Their size is approximately 1.9 x 1.3 inches.

- Blue-winged Teals favor curltop ladysthumb, barnyard grasses, and Pennsylvania smartweed in their diet.

- Male Blue-winged Teals frequently utter a peeping whistle or *keck-keck-keck*; females emit a quack similar to that of a Mallard but softer and more rapid.

- The average life span of adult male and female Blue-winged Teals is 1.9 and 1.5 years, respectively. The maximum known age for a wild banded Blue-winged Teal is 22 years.

- In the Mississippi Flyway, Blue-winged Teals ranked fifth in number of ducks harvested during 1991–1995 with an average of about 314,000 taken each year.

- Blue-winged Teals are the first migrant duck species to appear in the fall, sometimes as soon as late July, and the last to head northward in the spring.

- Generally, the highest number of Blue-winged Teals in the Illinois River and central Mississippi River regions is less than 30,000; they are more abundant in the Illinois River valley.

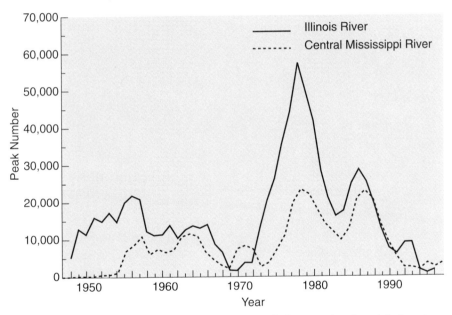

Figure 7. *Three-year moving average of peak numbers of Blue-winged Teals aerially inventoried during fall in the Illinois River and the central Mississippi River regions, 1948–1996.*

- **Average Date of the Peak Fall Migration by Aerial Inventory Region** (see map, page 10)

Illinois River Region	8–14 Sep.
Central Mississippi River Region	15–21 Sep.
Northeast Region	1–14 Sep.

Green-winged Teal
(Greenwing)
Anas crecca

- The breeding adult male Green-winged Teal has a chestnut-colored head with an iridescent green face patch sweeping backward from the eye. A vertical white stripe extends from the shoulder to the breast. The female is mottled

Female and male   TOM HUMBURG

brown with a dark eyeline, and in early fall males resemble females. A green speculum is usually visible in both sexes. The flight of the Green-winged Teal is generally low and erratic with the entire flock twisting and turning as a unit.

- Recently, Green-winged Teals have been recorded nesting in five counties (Cook, Grundy, Kane, Macoupin, Mason) in Illinois.

- Important foods for Green-winged Teals in Illinois are redroot flatsedge and ferruginous flatsedge.

- Males have a clear, short, often repeated whistle; females have an airy diffuse quack.

- The maximum known age for a wild banded Green-winged Teal is 20 years.

- The Green-winged Teal ranked third in number of ducks harvested in Illinois during 1991 to 1995 with an average of about 14,500 taken each year; in the Mississippi Flyway it also ranked third with an average of 342,000 harvested per year.

- Peak numbers indicate that Green-winged Teals were more abundant during fall in the Illinois River region than in the central Mississippi River region.

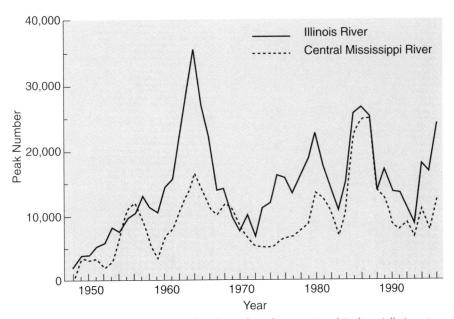

Figure 8. *Three-year moving average of peak numbers of Green-winged Teals aerially inventoried during fall in the Illinois River and the central Mississippi River regions, 1948–1996.*

- **Average Date of the Peak Fall Migration by Aerial Inventory Region** (see map, page 10)

Illinois River Region	27 Oct.–2 Nov.
Central Mississippi River Region	27 Oct.–2 Nov.
Northeast Region	13–26 Oct.
Southern Mississippi River Region	13–26 Oct.
Reservoirs in Central and Southern Illinois	13–26 Oct.
Cooling Lakes in Central and Southern Illinois	27 Oct.–9 Nov.

American Wigeon
(Baldpate)
Anas americana

- The breeding adult male American Wigeon has a white crown with green bands on either side extending from the eye to the back of the head. The head of the female is grayish, which contrasts with the pale gray-brown sides and chest. Both sexes have a pale blue dark-tipped bill. In flight, a large rectangular white patch is visible on the upper wing of both sexes. The American Wigeon is a nervous bird. Its flight is fast and irregular. When flying in a flock, their movements may be compared with those of pigeons.

Female and male   Tom Humburg

- American Wigeons are rare nesters in Illinois.

- Muskgrass and corn are two important foods of American Wigeons in Illinois.

- The male vocalizes three clear whistling notes (*whew-whew-whew*), with the middle note pitched higher than the other two; the female utters an infrequent low quacking note.

- The estimated average life span of adult American Wigeons is 2.3 years for males and 1.7 years for females. The maximum known age for a wild banded American Wigeon is 21 years.

- Typically, a peak population of less than 100,000 American Wigeons occurs in the Illinois River region and the central Mississippi River region. Since 1987, peak numbers have been fewer than 60,000.

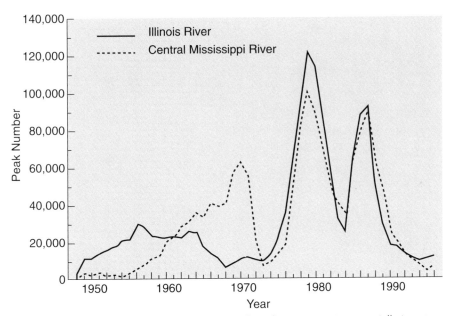

Figure 9. *Three-year moving average of peak numbers of American Wigeons aerially invento-ried during fall in the Illinois River and the central Mississippi River regions, 1948–1996.*

- Average Date of the Peak Fall Migration by Aerial Inventory
  Region (see map, page 10)

Illinois River Region	27 Oct.–2 Nov.
Central Mississippi River Region	20 Oct.–26 Oct.
Northeast Region	13 Oct.–9 Nov.
Southern Mississippi River Region	27 Oct.–9 Nov.
Reservoirs and Cooling Lakes	
in Central and Southern Illinois	27 Oct.–9 Nov.

Male   TOM HUMBURG

Female   TOM HUMBURG

Gadwall
(Gray Duck)
Anas strepera

- The adult male Gadwall breeding plumage is black on the upper and lower tail coverts (the feathers covering the bases of the longer main feathers on the tail) with a white speculum. The female has a uniformly mottled brown body, dark tail feathers and white speculum. The narrow gray bill, edged with orange, helps distinguish the female Gadwall from the female Mallard. Gadwalls have chestnut-colored feathers on the shoulder that are more noticeable in adults than in immatures. Gadwalls usually fly in a direct line in small, compact flocks. They have a rapid wing beat.

- Gadwalls were historically rare nesters in Illinois. Recently they have been recorded nesting in five counties (Cass, LaSalle, Mason, Morgan, Schuyler).

- The most important food items for Gadwalls in Illinois are brittle naiad, fennelleaf pondweed, duckweed, and common arrowhead.

- The male has a *kack-kack* and whistle sound; the female has a soft, Mallardlike quack.

- The maximum known age for a wild banded Gadwall is 19 years.

- The Gadwall ranked fourth in number of ducks harvested in Illinois during 1991 to 1995 with an average of about 11,500 each year. It also ranked fourth in number of ducks harvested in the Mississippi Flyway with an average of approximately 330,000 taken each year.

- Usually, peak numbers of fewer than 20,000 Gadwalls occur in the Illinois River and central Mississippi River regions, but fall numbers have been increasing in recent years.

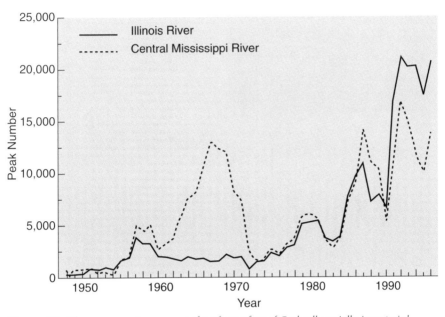

Figure 10. *Three-year moving average of peak numbers of Gadwalls aerially inventoried during fall in the Illinois River and the central Mississippi River regions, 1948–1996.*

- Average Date of the Peak Fall Migration by Aerial Inventory Region (see map, page 10)

Illinois River Region	27 Oct.–2 Nov.
Central Mississippi River Region	27 Oct.–2 Nov.
Northeast Region	13–26 Oct.
Southern Mississippi River Region	10–23 Nov.
Reservoirs in Central and Southern Illinois	27 Oct.–9 Nov.
Cooling Lakes in Central and Southern Illinois	10–23 Nov.

Female and male   Tom Humburg

Northern Shoveler
(Spoonbill)
Anas clypeata

- Northern Shovelers have a large shovel-like bill that is longer than the head. Breeding adult males have a dark green head and neck, a white belly, and rust-red flanks. The body of the female is a drab mottled brown with white wing linings. Both sexes have a green speculum and blue-gray upperwing coverts although these features are less prominent in females. The flight of the Northern Shoveler is steady and direct.

- Northern Shovelers have been recorded nesting in only eight counties (Cook, DeKalb, DuPage, Fulton, Grundy, McHenry, Madison, Mason) in Illinois since 1930.

- Northern Shovelers consume invertebrates and plant seeds, but their large bills are also used to filter plankton from the water surface and the surface of bottom soils in shallow water.

- The maximum known age for a wild banded Northern Shoveler is 16 years.

- The colorful males have a low raspy chuckle, seldom heard except in spring; the female quacks similar to a Mallard, but softer.

- Although their numbers have increased in recent years, generally peak populations of fewer than 8,000 spoonbills have occurred during fall in the Illinois River and central Mississippi River regions.

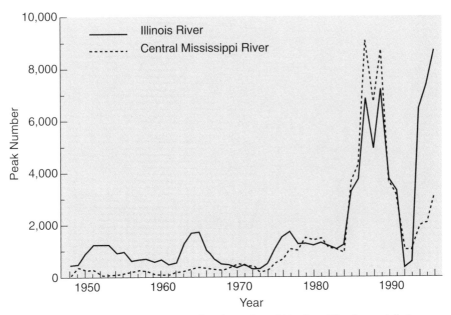

Figure 11. *Three-year moving average of peak numbers of Northern Shovelers aerially inventoried during fall in the Illinois River and the central Mississippi River regions, 1948–1996.*

- **Average Date of the Peak Fall Migration by Aerial Inventory Region** (see map, page 10)

Illinois River Region	27 Oct.–2 Nov.
Central Mississippi River Region	27 Oct.–2 Nov.
Northeast Region	13–26 Oct.
Southern Mississippi River Region	27 Oct.–9 Nov.
Reservoirs and Cooling Lakes in Central and Southern Illinois	27 Oct.–9 Nov.

TOM HUMBURG

A small flock of mostly male Northern Shovelers swimming in a marsh.

Perching Ducks

Female and male   DAVE MENKE

Wood Duck
(Woodie, Summer Duck)
Aix sponsa

- The beautifully crested male Wood Duck is patterned in iridescent greens, purples, and blues with a distinctive white chin patch. It has two white parallel lines, one starting from the base of its bill and the other from the back of its red eye and stretching to the rear of its crest. The bill is red with a white patch on top. The female has a slightly crested head and is mostly grayish brown with a grayer head and neck. There is an elliptical white patch around the eye.

- Wood Ducks are the most abundant species of breeding ducks in Illinois, nesting in every county. The average breeding population estimate is 1.7 ducks per square mile of the state. Wood Ducks initiate nests in early March and finish nesting in July. Occasionally they raise two broods in one season. Wood Ducks exhibit a high degree of fidelity to nesting areas, and a large percentage of females have been recorded returning to the same nesting area year after year. They nest in tree cavities or artificial nest boxes, sometimes at a considerable distance from water. A lining of down is the only nest material added to the cavity. Eggs are a dull white approximately 2.0 x 1.5 inches. Clutch size averages 12 eggs, and incubation ranges from 28 to 37 days.

- The most important foods for Wood Ducks in Illinois are pin oak acorns and corn.

- The handsome males have a soft ascending *ter-we-ee*, heard while flock feeding and at roost sites; females produce a distinctive squealing *wee-e-e-e-ek* or *woo-e-e-e-ek* alarm call.

- The mean life span of adult male and female Wood Ducks is approximately 1.7 and 1.4 years, respectively. The maximum known age for a wild banded Wood Duck is 22 years.

- The Wood Duck was probably the most abundant duck in the United States east of the Mississippi River during the early nineteenth century. Populations were drastically reduced by human activities, but their numbers have rebounded in recent decades.

- The Wood Duck ranked second in number of ducks harvested in Illinois from 1991 to 1995 with an average of approximately 31,000 taken each year. In the Mississippi Flyway it also ranked second with an average of about 554,000 harvested each year.

- Wood Ducks readily accept artificial nest structures, and the appropriate deployment and care of these structures can enhance local populations.

- Wood Ducks are not easily inventoried from the air because of their secretive nature and preference for dense bottomland forest. Consequently, they are not recorded on the Illinois Natural History Survey's aerial inventories.

MICHELLE GEORGI

Male Wood Duck standing on a nest box while the female views the surroundings from the entrance.

TOM HUMBURG

Male and female Wood Duck loafing on a log.

Diving Ducks

Males   T OM H UMBURG

Female   T OM H UMBURG

Lesser Scaup
(Bluebill)
Aythya affinis

- The adult male Lesser Scaup has a pale blue bill with a black tip. It has a black chest and rump, blackish peaked head, and pale gray back. The back of the female is dark brown with gray-brown flanks. The brown head of the female is also peaked with a small white patch at the base of the bill. In flight, a short white wing stripe is visible on both sexes. Lesser Scaups usually fly in compact groups with rapid, often erratic movements.

- Lesser Scaups rarely nest in Illinois, but they have been recorded nesting in four counties (Cass, Fulton, LaSalle, Mason) in recent decades.

- As is the case for many other species of diving ducks, invertebrates, including fingernail clams, freshwater snails, and freshwater clams, are an important food of Lesser Scaups in Illinois.

- Courting male Lesser Scaups utter a soft *whee-ooo*. Males may emit loud whistles, deep scolding notes, and loud *scaup* calls when alarmed. They are generally silent in winter. Females are silent much of the time but utter a soft, purring *br-r-r-r-r-rp* when they call. Females are most prone to call when in flight.

- The maximum known age for a wild banded Lesser Scaup is 18 years.

- Numbers of Lesser Scaups have decreased during fall migration in the Illinois River valley, a result of the loss of invertebrates in such historical feeding areas as Peoria Lake. Unfortunately, and for unknown reasons, numbers of Lesser Scaups also decreased in recent years along the Mississippi River on important migration areas such as Pool 19.

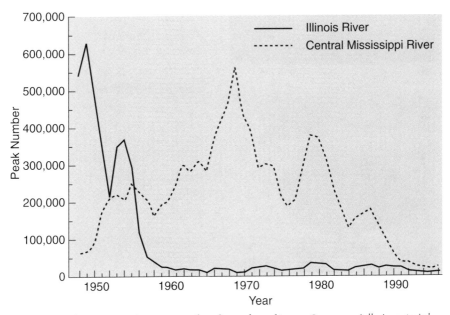

Figure 12. *Three-year moving average of peak numbers of Lesser Scaups aerially inventoried during fall in the Illinois River and the central Mississippi River regions, 1948-1996.*

- Average Date of the Peak Fall Migration by Aerial Inventory Region (see map, page 10)

Illinois River Region	10–16 Nov.
Central Mississippi River Region	3–9 Nov.
Northeast Region	27 Oct.–9 Nov.
Southern Mississippi River Region	27 Oct.–9 Nov.
Reservoirs and Cooling Lakes in Central and Southern Illinois	27 Oct.–9 Nov.

Canvasback
(Can)
Aythya valisineria

Male   Tom Humburg

Female   Tom Humburg

- The breeding adult male Canvasback has a chestnut-red head and neck, a black breast and bill, and white sides, belly, and back. The eye is red. Females have a sandy-brown head and neck with a grayish back. A distinctive characteristic of both sexes is the broadly sloping forehead and long black bill. Canvasbacks are among the fastest flying ducks. A group of Canvasbacks will shift from flying in waving lines to temporary Vs.

- Canvasbacks rarely nest in Illinois.

- They feed on aquatic vegetation, such as American wild celery, but eat fingernail clams in the absence of aquatic vegetation.

- Canvasbacks are largely silent except during spring courtship. The regal males grunt or croak; females quack and have a low, guttural, purring call.

- The maximum known age for a wild banded Canvasback is 22 years.

- Canvasbacks have been periodically protected from hunting in recent decades because of low continental populations. During migration, Canvasbacks are most abundant in Illinois along the Mississippi River, principally Pool 19. Their numbers in Peoria Lake and elsewhere in the Illinois River valley have not rebounded since the loss of aquatic plants there in the 1950s.

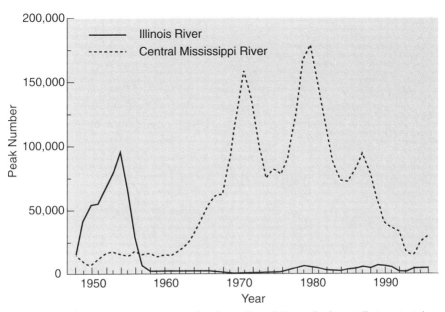

Figure 13. *Three-year moving average of peak numbers of Canvasbacks aerially inventoried during fall in the Illinois River and the central Mississippi River regions, 1948–1996.*

- Average Date of the Peak Fall Migration by Aerial Inventory Region (see map, page 10)

Illinois River Region	10–16 Nov.
Central Mississippi River Region	24–30 Nov.
Northeast Region	27 Oct.–9 Nov.
Southern Mississippi River Region	8–21 Dec.
Reservoirs in Central and Southern Illinois	27 Oct.– 9 Nov.
Cooling Lakes in Central and Southern Illinois	24 Nov.–7 Dec.

GEORGE ARTHUR
The regal and dynamic Canvasback in flight.

Waterfowl and Coots Common to Illinois   43

Ring-necked Duck
(Blackjack, Ringbill)
Aythya collaris

Males in center.   Tom Humburg

- The breeding adult male Ring-necked Duck has a black back with a white, vertical mark on the sides of the breast. The head is shaped high and angular. The female Ring-necked Duck is dark gray-brown with a pale eye ring and a line behind the eye. The bill of both sexes is gray with a white ring and black tip. The faint brown ring on a male Ring-necked Duck's neck is not easily seen in the field, but the light bands at the tip and base of the bill are conspicuous.

- Ring-necked Ducks are rare nesters in Illinois.

- The most important foods of Ring-necked Ducks in Illinois include common hornwort, leafy pondweed, water star grass, and duckweed. Ring-necked Ducks, like Redheads and Canvasbacks, are diving ducks that prefer aquatic vegetation when it is available rather than invertebrates.

- Ring-necked Ducks are largely silent except during spring courtship. Males grunt or croak; females quack and have a low, guttural, purring call.

- The average life span of adult male and female Ring-necked Ducks is 2.8 and 1.3 years, respectively. The maximum known age for a wild banded Ring-necked Duck is 20 years.

- The Ring-necked Duck ranked fifth in number of ducks harvested in Illinois from 1991 to 1995 with an average of about 9,400 taken each year.

- Reasonable numbers of Ring-necked Ducks occur in the Illinois River and central Mississippi River regions during fall.

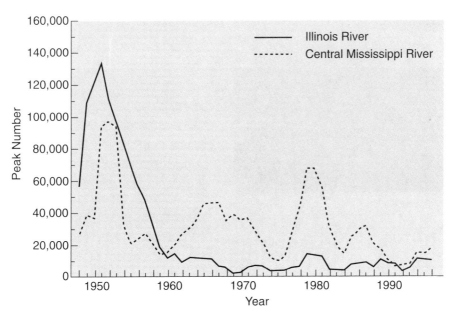

Figure 14. *Three-year moving average of peak numbers of Ring-necked Ducks aerially inventoried during fall in the Illinois River and central Mississippi River regions, 1948–1996.*

- **Average Date of the Peak Fall Migration by Aerial Inventory Region** (see map, page 10)

Illinois River Region	27 Oct.–2 Nov.
Central Mississippi River Region	27 Oct.–2 Nov.
Northeast Region	27 Oct.–9 Nov.
Southern Mississippi River Region	27 Oct.–9 Nov.
Reservoirs and Cooling Lakes in Central and Southern Illinois	27 Oct.–9 Nov.

Male and female   TOM HUMBURG

Redhead
(Pochard)
Aythya americana

- The breeding adult male Redhead has a chestnut-red head and yellow eyes. The breast is black with a gray back and white belly. The long black-tipped, blue-gray bill is noticeable in both sexes. The female has a tawny brown head and body. This duck is often seen with the Canvasback.

- Redheads are uncommon nesters in Illinois; however, they have been recorded nesting in six counties (Cass, Cook, Lake, Madison, Mason, Morgan) in Illinois since 1930. Some female Redheads lay eggs in nests of other ducks and American Coots— a practice referred to as nest parasitism.

- Recent food habit studies indicate that the most important food items for Redheads in Illinois are midge larvae, fingernail clams, burrowing mayflies, dragonfly nymphs, and pondweed vegetation. Redheads generally favor a diet of aquatic vegetation, which is lacking in many Illinois wetlands today.

- Redheads are largely silent except during spring courtship. Males have a distinctive almost catlike *meow*; females have a harsh *squak*.

- The maximum known age for a wild banded Redhead is 21 years.

- More Redheads utilize the large water areas of the central Mississippi River region than the Illinois River region during fall.

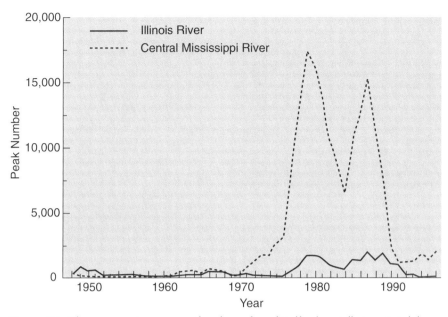

Figure 15. *Three-year moving average of peak numbers of Redheads aerially inventoried during fall in the Illinois River and the central Mississippi River regions, 1948–1996.*

- **Average Date of the Peak Fall Migration by Aerial Inventory Region** (see map, page 10)

Illinois River Region	3–9 Nov.
Central Mississippi River Region	17–23 Nov.
Northeast Region	27 Oct.–9 Nov.
Southern Mississippi River Region	10–23 Nov.
Reservoirs in Central and Southern Illinois	10–23 Nov.
Cooling Lakes in Central and Southern Illinois	27 Oct.–9 Nov.

Tom Humburg

A pair of Redheads in a wetland.

Ruddy Duck
(Butterball)
Oxyura jamaicensis

Male   Tom Humburg

Female   Tom Humburg

- The breeding adult male Ruddy Duck has a bright blue bill, black cap, and white cheeks, which distinguish it from other ducks. Plumage and bill color in fall and winter are drab compared with their colors in spring. The female has a dusky brown-grayish body. The head has a dark cap with a dark line across the pale cheek. Ruddy Ducks often dive or swim away from danger rather than fly. When flying, these chunky bodied ducks move their small wings so fast that they resemble bumblebees. Males cock their stiff tails upright at an angle and are the only species to habitually do so.

- Although they are rare nesters in Illinois, Ruddy Ducks were reported nesting in three counties before 1930 and in nine counties (Cook, Douglas, DuPage, Jackson, Kane, Lake, Madison, Mason, Union) since then.

- Dragonfly nymphs and duckweed are two important foods of Ruddy Ducks in Illinois.

- Ruddy Ducks are silent most of the year but utter a few low nasal clucking sounds during the breeding season.

- The maximum known age for a wild banded Ruddy Duck is 13 years.

- Generally, fewer than 5,000 Ruddy Ducks occur during fall in the Illinois River region and central Mississippi River region.

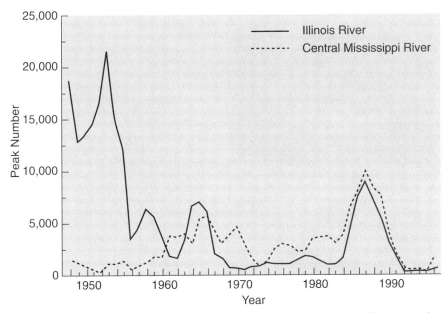

Figure 16. *Three-year moving average of peak numbers of Ruddy Ducks aerially inventoried during fall in the Illinois River and the central Mississippi River regions, 1948–1996.*

- Average Date of the Peak Fall Migration by Aerial Inventory Region (see map, page 10)

Illinois River Region	27 Oct.–2 Nov., 10–16 Nov.
Central Mississippi River Region	27 Oct.–2 Nov.
Northeast Region	27 Oct.–9 Nov.
Southern Mississippi River Region	10–23 Nov.
Reservoirs in Central and Southern Illinois	10–23 Nov.
Cooling Lakes in Central and Southern Illinois	27 Oct.–9 Nov., 24 Nov.–7 Dec.

A *male Ruddy Duck resting in cattails.*
Tom Humburg

Common Goldeneye

(Whistler)

Bucephala clangula

Male   HARRY LUMSDEN

Female   HARRY LUMSDEN

- The breeding adult male Common Goldeneye has a glossy greenish head with white round spots between the eyes and the bill. The eyes are a bright amber. The back is black with white on the sides. The female has a brown head with a dark-colored bill that is tipped with yellow in spring. Both sexes have black wings with a large white patch. Common Goldeneyes are active, strong flyers moving singly or in small flocks.

- Only one instance of a Common Goldeneye nesting in Illinois has been reported. They usually nest in tree cavities.

- During courtship, males emit a nasal rasping *peent* call. In flight, Common Goldeneyes make a whistling sound that actually emanates from their wings.

- The maximum known age for a wild banded Common Goldeneye is 14 years.

- Common Goldeneyes are among the latest arrivals during fall migration in Illinois. They are found frequently on large rivers and on large ice-free bodies of water. In some years, as many as 30,000 Common Goldeneyes have occurred in the Illinois River and central Mississippi River regions during fall.

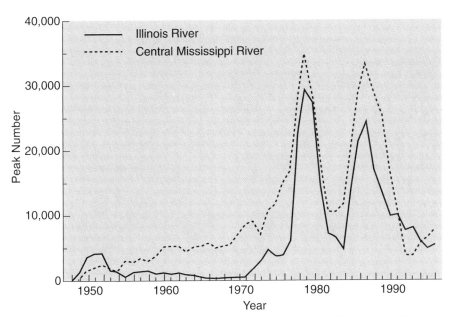

Figure 17. *Three-year moving average of peak numbers of Common Goldeneyes aerially inventoried during fall in the Illinois River and the central Mississippi River regions, 1948–1996.*

- Average Date of the Peak Fall Migration by Aerial Inventory Region (see map, page 10)

Illinois River Region   8–14 Dec.
Central Mississippi River Region   8–14 Dec.

Female on left.   Tom Humburg

Common Merganser
(Goosander, Sawbill, Fish Duck)
Mergus merganser

- The Common Merganser is one of the largest ducks. The breeding adult male has a narrow red bill with sawlike teeth along the edges and a glossy dark green head. When in flight, much white on the upper wing can be seen. The female has a white chin and brown head with a ragged crest. Her wings sport a white speculum. The color division between the head and white breast is sharp on both sexes. A flock flies in a "follow-the-leader" style.

- Common Mergansers do not nest in Illinois.

- The ice-free, warm waters of power plant cooling lakes are a favorite area of Common Mergansers; their diet is principally fishes.

- Common Mergansers are usually silent; sometimes they emit low *qua-auk*, guttural calls or hisses.

- The maximum known age for a banded Common Merganser is 13 years.

- Common Mergansers are the latest arriving species of ducks during fall migration; their appearance signifies the end of the fall migration of ducks through Illinois and announces that winter is generally imminent. Peak populations of fewer than 14,000 Common Mergansers are found during fall in the Illinois River and central Mississippi River regions.

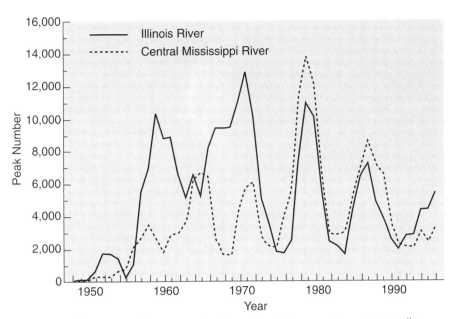

Figure 18. *Three-year moving average of peak numbers of Common Mergansers aerially inventoried during fall in the Illinois River and the central Mississippi River regions, 1948–1996.*

- **Average Date of the Peak for Fall Migration by Aerial Inventory Region** (see map, page 10)

  Illinois River Region   15–21 Dec.
  Central Mississippi River Region   15–21 Dec.

Male on left. Tom Humburg

Hooded Merganser
(Sawbill, Fish Duck)
Lophodytes cucullatus

- Breeding adult male Hooded Mergansers have narrow, black, serrated bills and a black, rounded crest with a prominent white patch starting behind the yellow eye. This crest forms the "hood" for which they are named and can be flattened or expanded dramatically. The brown head of the female has a rust orange tinge on the crest. Only a small portion of white shows on the female speculum. Both sexes have a dark back. The Hooded Merganser is usually seen in pairs or small flocks. Their rapid wing strokes give an impression of great speed.

- Hooded Mergansers have been recorded nesting in 36 counties in Illinois, generally in March and April. They nest in tree cavities or nest boxes in wooded areas near water and line their cavities with down. Eggs are white and number 7 to 13 with a size of about 2.1 x 1.7 inches. The eggs are larger and more oval than those of Wood Ducks. Their incubation period is about 32 days.

- Their diet is principally small fishes and aquatic invertebrates.

- The courting male emits a froglike *crooo* and a rolling, croaking note.

- The maximum known age for a wild banded Hooded Merganser is 11 years.

- Small numbers of Hooded Mergansers are seen on aerial inventories throughout Illinois.

Coots

STEPHEN HAVERA

American Coot
(Mudhen, Ricehen)
Fulica americana

- Both the male and female American Coot have a black head and neck and a slate-colored stocky body. The sides of the lower tail coverts are white. The white bill has a red ring near the tip and a red bulge on top of the frontal shield. The legs are greenish or grayish. Before becoming airborne, American Coots patter across the water on lobed feet, giving them an awkward appearance. They are weak flyers.

- American Coots have recently nested in 29 counties in Illinois. They build their nests in clumps of emergent wetland vegetation, such as cattails, on or near shore. The eggs are tan with black speckles and number 6 to 16 with a size of about 1.8 x 1.3 inches.

- Their diet is largely plant foods.

- American Coots emit a grating *kuk-kuk-kuk-kuk* sound and various other short rough notes, cackles, clucks, and croaks.

- The maximum known age for a wild banded American Coot is 22 years.

- Several thousand American Coots appear each fall in the Illinois River and central Mississippi River regions and are more abundant than many species of waterfowl.

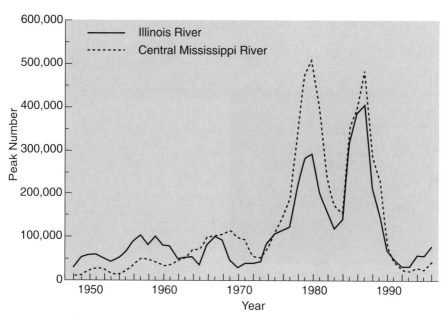

Figure 19. *Three-year moving average of peak numbers of American Coots aerially inventoried during fall in the Illinois River and the central Mississippi River regions, 1948–1996.*

- **Average Date of the Peak Fall Migration by Aerial Inventory Region** (see map, page 10)

Illinois River Region	27 Oct.–2 Nov.
Central Mississippi River Region	27 Oct.–2 Nov.
Northeast Region	13–26 Oct.
Southern Mississippi River Region	27 Oct.–9 Nov.
Reservoirs and Cooling Lakes in Central and Southern Illinois	27 Oct.–9 Nov.

Geese

MICHELLE GEORGI

Canada Goose
(Honker, Canada)
Branta canadensis

- The bill, head, neck, legs, and feet of all races are black; there is also a distinct white cheek patch that usually covers the throat. The back and wings are usually gray-brown to dark brown with a white V-shaped bar above the black tail. The sides and breast are dull gray to dark brown.

- Canada Geese are monogamous and mate for life. Both parents aid in raising the goslings. Giant Canada Geese are adaptable to a variety of environments—more than any other race of Canada Geese. Once thought to be extinct, they are now permanent residents in Illinois and nest in all 102 counties. Giant Canada Geese begin nesting in March in Illinois, with an average clutch of 6 eggs. Incubation time ranges from 25 to 30 days. They have an average of about 4 goslings per pair. Goslings usually fledge at 8 weeks. Giant Canada Geese nest in scraped-out depressions on the ground, in artificial nesting structures near or over water, and on small islands and muskrat lodges. Nests are made of weeds and grass and lined with down. Eggs are a buff or drab white with a size of about 3.5 x 2.5 inches.

ROBERT MONTGOMERY

Giant Canada Geese readily accept artificial nest structures.

- Young winter wheat plants and corn are important foods for Canada Geese wintering in southern Illinois.

- The call of the Canada Goose ranges from the resonant *uh-whonk* of the larger races to the yelping, high-pitched *unc* of the smaller ones. Larger races usually utter longer, less frequent, more sonorous calls.

- Canada Geese fly in the familiar V formation.

- The maximum known age for a wild banded Canada Goose is 24 years.

- Illinois hosts thousands of individuals from the migrant Mississippi Valley Population of Canada Geese during fall, winter, and early spring. Numbers of Canada Geese frequenting the Illinois River and central Mississippi River regions have increased in recent decades as the Mississippi Valley Population and the number of Giant Canada Geese have grown.

MICHELLE GEORGI

A flock of Canada Geese coming in for a landing.

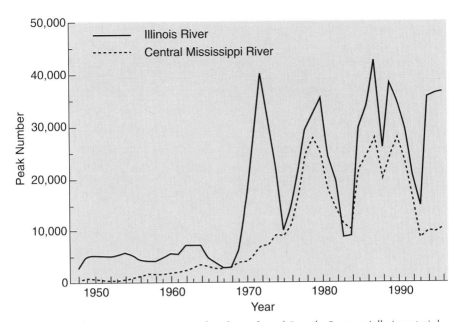

Figure 20. *Three-year moving average of peak numbers of Canada Geese aerially inventoried during fall in the Illinois River and the central Mississippi River regions, 1948–1996.*

- **Average Date of the Peak Fall Migration by Aerial Inventory Region** (see map, page 10)

Illinois River Region	27 Oct.–2 Nov., 8–14 Dec.
Central Mississippi River Region	8–14 Dec.
Northeast Region	27 Oct.–9 Nov.

STEPHEN HAVERA

Lesser Snow Goose
(Snow, Blue, Wavie)
Chen caerulescens

- The Lesser Snow Goose appears in one of two color phases: a dark plumage (known as the blue goose) and a white plumage (known as the snow goose). Originally, the two were thought to be separate races; they are now considered two different color phases of the same race. Both color phases are present in Illinois during spring and fall.

- Lesser Snow Geese nest in the high Arctic of North America.

- Lesser Snow Geese are herbivores that graze and frequently "grub" tubers and roots from the soil.

- Lesser Snow Geese are generally the most vocal of waterfowl. The call is a shrill, scratchy *uh-uk*, somewhat similar to the yelp of a fox terrier.

- Lesser Snow Geese fly in a loose V or wavy formation.

- The maximum known age for a wild banded Lesser Snow Goose is 26 years.

- Usually fewer than 25,000 Lesser Snow Geese occur during fall in the Illinois River and central Mississippi River regions.

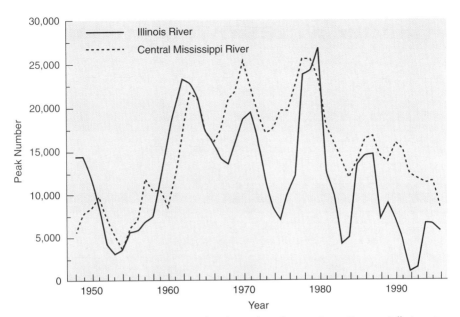

Figure 21. *Three-year moving average of peak numbers of Lesser Snow Geese aerially inventoried during fall in the Illinois River and the central Mississippi River regions, 1948–1996.*

- **Average Date of the Peak Fall Migration by Aerial Inventory Region** (see map, page 10)

Illinois River Region	27 Oct.–2 Nov.
Central Mississippi River Region	10–16 Nov.
Northeast Region	27 Oct.–9 Nov.
Southern Mississippi River Region	8–21 Dec.
Reservoirs in Central and Southern Illinois	10–23 Nov.
Cooling Lakes in Central and Southern Illinois	27 Oct.–9 Nov.

EIGHT
Illinois Waterfowl Milestones

1865   The first Illinois water-
        fowl season was
        established.

1903   The first bag limit (50
        ducks) was established
        in Illinois.

1909   The practice of baiting
        for waterfowl hunting
        was restricted in Illinois.

1913   The Federal Migratory
        Bird Law, the first
        federal migratory bird
        hunting regulation, was
        enacted. It limited the
        length of the hunting
        season for waterfowl.

TOM HUMBURG

A hen and drake Mallard taking flight.

1913   Spring hunting of waterfowl in Illinois was eliminated.

1914   Wood Ducks were protected in Illinois.

1918   The first Canada Goose season was established in Illinois with
        a bag limit of 8.

1918   The Migratory Bird Treaty Act was passed by the federal
        government. It formulated hunting season times and lengths,
        daily bag limits, and hunting areas. It protected Wood Ducks
        and eiders and prohibited spring shooting and market hunting.

1924   The Upper Mississippi River Wildlife and Fish Refuge (Great
        River Refuge) was established along a 284-mile stretch of the
        Mississippi River between Wabasha, Minnesota, and Rock
        Island, Illinois. This was the first time Congress provided
        funds to purchase a general wildlife refuge.

1927   The first public refuge in Illinois was established at Horseshoe
        Lake Wildlife Management Area by the Illinois Department of
        Conservation. Its primary role has been to provide wintering
        habitat for Canada Geese.

1934   The Migratory Bird Hunting Stamp Act (federal duck stamp) was enacted.

1935   The use of baiting and live decoys for the hunting of waterfowl was prohibited by the federal government.

1937   The Pittman-Robertson Act created the Federal Aid in Wildlife Restoration Program that allocated funds generated from excise taxes on the sale of sporting arms and ammunition, archery equipment, and handguns to the states for use in acquiring and managing wildlife habitat or supporting associated research.

MAX SCHNORF

A bottomland lake in the Illinois River valley.

1937   Ducks Unlimited was established.

1943   Rice Lake Fish and Wildlife Area in the Illinois River valley was the first state refuge established for ducks.

1959   After several closings and reopenings, the Wood Duck season was opened in the Mississippi Flyway with a bag limit of one.

1975   The Illinois Duck Stamp Program was established.

1977   Nontoxic shot for hunting waterfowl was required in six counties of Illinois.

1985   The 1985 Food Security Act (Farm Bill) was enacted establishing programs for controlling soil erosion and providing wildlife habitat (Conservation Reserve Program) and protecting wetlands (Swampbuster).

1986   The North American Waterfowl Management Plan was signed by the United States and Canada setting a 15-year action agenda to ensure the survival of waterfowl populations and to enhance and protect high-quality wetland habitat.

1991   Nationwide use of nontoxic shot for hunting waterfowl was implemented.

NINE

Observing Waterbirds

Waterfowl and other waterbirds may be observed throughout fall and spring migrations during unrestricted periods on a number of public areas in Illinois. Many species of ducks can be seen in several areas. Goose Point Lookout over Spring Lake in the Savanna Fish and Wildlife Refuge is easily accessible in the northern part of the state. Chautauqua National Wildlife Refuge in central Illinois hosts numerous shorebirds and several thousands of geese and ducks, particularly dabbling ducks including Mallards, Northern Pintails, and American Wigeons. Pool 19 (Keokuk Pool) of the Mississippi River attracts large numbers of diving ducks, especially Canvasbacks, Lesser Scaups, and Ring-necked Ducks, which can be seen along the Great River Road (State Route 96) between Hamilton and Nauvoo. Canada Geese can be appreciated on their traditional wintering areas of Crab Orchard National Wildlife Refuge and Union County and Horseshoe Lake wildlife management areas in southern Illinois.

Detailed information about observing waterbirds at sites in Illinois noted on the accompanying map and key can be acquired by contacting specific locations. For state areas, see the Department of Natural Resources home page (http://dnr.state.il.us/) or call the Public Information Officer (217–785–0970). Federal refuge information may be obtained from the Regional Public Affairs Office (612–725–3520). Additional information for viewing waterfowl can be found in the Suggested Reading section under the heading "Waterfowl Observation and Identification" on page 70.

MICHELLE GEORGI

Ducks utilizing an impoundment managed for moist-soil plants.

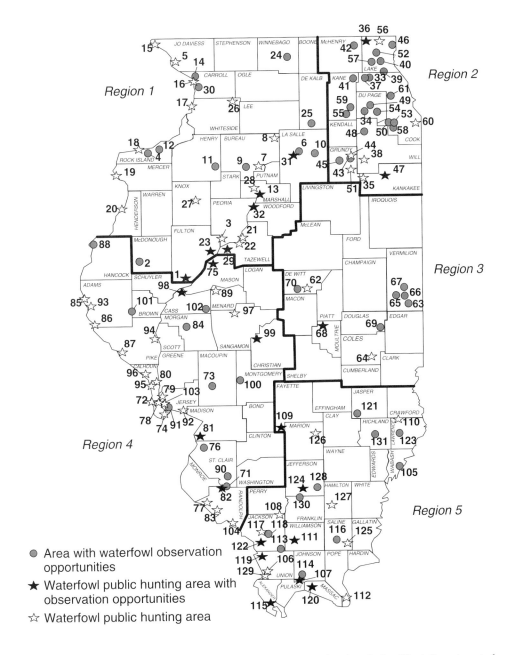

- ● Area with waterfowl observation opportunities
- ★ Waterfowl public hunting area with observation opportunities
- ☆ Waterfowl public hunting area

Figure 22. *Waterfowl observation and public hunting areas located within the five Illinois Department of Natural Resources Regions (Summarized from DeLorme Mapping 1991, Illinois Department of Natural Resources 1996, Murphy and Mellen 1997, and Illinois Department of Conservation n.d.).*

Key to Waterfowl Observation
And Public Hunting Areas

REGION 1

1 Anderson Lake Fish and Wildlife Area
2 Argyle Lake State Park
3 Banner Marsh Fish and Wildlife Area
4 Blanchard Island Recreation Area
5 Blanding Wildlife Management Area, Federal Land
6 Buffalo Rock State Park
7 DePue Fish and Wildlife Area
8 Donnelley Fish and Wildlife Area
9 Hennepin Canal State Park
10 Illini State Park
11 Johnson Sauk Trail State Park
12 Loud Thunder Forest Preserve
13 Marshall Fish and Wildlife Area
14 Mississippi Palisades State Park
15 Mississippi River Pool 12
16 Mississippi River Pool 13
17 Mississippi River Pool 14
18 Mississippi River Pool 16
19 Mississippi River Pool 17
20 Mississippi River Pool 18
21 Pekin Lake Fish and Wildlife Area
22 Powerton Lake Fish and Wildlife Area
23 Rice Lake Fish and Wildlife Area
24 Rock Cut State Park
25 Shabbona Lake State Recreation Area
26 Sinnissippi Lake
27 Snakeden Hollow Fish and Wildlife Area
28 Sparland Conservation Area
29 Spring Lake Conservation Area
30 Spring Lake Unit-Upper Mississippi River National Wildlife and Fish Refuge
31 Starved Rock State Park
32 Woodford County Fish and Wildlife Area

REGION 2

33 Baker's Lake
34 Blackwell Forest Preserve
35 Braidwood Lake Fish and Wildlife Area
36 Chain-O-Lakes State Park
37 Crabtree Nature Center
38 Des Plaines Conservation Area
39 Des Plaines River Greenway
40 Edward L. Ryerson Conservation Area
41 Fox River Shores
42 Glacial Park
43 Goose Lake Prairie State Natural Area
44 Heidecke Lake Fish and Wildlife Area
45 Illinois and Michigan Canal
46 Illinois Beach State Park
47 Kankakee River State Park
48 Lake Renwick Forest Preserve
49 Lincoln Marsh Natural Area
50 Little Red Schoolhouse Nature Center
51 Mazonia Fish and Wildlife Area
52 McDonald Woods Forest Preserve
53 McGinnis Slough
54 Morton Arboretum
55 Red Oak Nature Center
56 Redwing Slough/Deer Lake State Natural Area
57 Reed-Turner Woodland Nature Preserve
58 Swallow Cliff Woods
59 Tekakwitha Woods
60 William A. Powers Conservation Area
61 Wolf Road Prairie Nature Preserve

REGION 3

62 Clinton Lake State Recreation Area
63 Forest Glen County Preserve
64 Fox Ridge State Park
65 Kennebuk County Park
66 Kickapoo State Park
67 Middlefork Fish and Wildlife Area
68 Shelbyville Fish and Wildlife Area
69 Walnut Point Fish and Wildlife Area
70 Weldon Springs State Park

REGION 4

71 Baldwin Lake
72 Batchtown Waterfowl Area

73 Beaver Dam State Park
74 Calhoun Point Waterfowl Area
75 Chautauqua National
Wildlife Refuge
76 Frank Holten State Park
77 Ft. de Chartres Historical Site
78 Fuller Lake Waterfowl Area
79 Glades-12 Mile Island
Waterfowl Area
80 Godar-Diamond-Hurricane Island
Waterfowl Area
81 Horseshoe Lake State Park
(Madison County)
82 Kaskaskia River Fish and
Wildlife Area
83 Kidd Lake State Natural Area
84 Leonard Wildlife Sanctuary
85 Mississippi River Pool 21
(Bear Creek and Long Island)
86 Mississippi River Pool 22
(Saverton Pool)
87 Mississippi River Pool 24
(Clarksville Pool)
88 Nauvoo Flat Wildlife Sanctuary
89 Oakford Conservation Area
90 Peabody King State Fish and
Wildlife Area
91 Pere Marquette State Park
92 Piasa Island Waterfowl Area
93 Quincy Bay Federal Land
94 Ray Norbut Fish and Wildlife Area
95 Red's Landing Waterfowl Area
96 Riprap Landing Waterfowl
Management Area
97 Sangamon County
Conservation Area
98 Sanganois Conservation Area
99 Sangchris Lake State Park
100 Shoal Creek Conservation Area
101 Siloam Springs State Park
102 Site M
103 Stump Lake Waterfowl Area
104 Turkey Bluffs Fish and Wildlife Area

REGION 5
105 Beall Woods Conservation Area
and Nature Preserve
106 Bluff Lakes Federal Land
107 Cache River State Natural Area
108 Campbell Pond
109 Carlyle Lake Wildlife
Management Area

110 Chauncey Marsh Natural Area
111 Crab Orchard National
Wildlife Refuge
112 Dog Island Wildlife
Management Area
113 Giant City State Park
114 Heron Pond Natural Area
115 Horseshoe Lake Wildlife
Management Area
(Alexander County)
116 J.N. Spanel Wetland Restoration
and Interpretive Site
117 Kinkaid Lake Fish and Wildlife Area
118 Lake Murphysboro State Park
119 LaRue Swamp Federal Land
120 Mermet Lake Fish and Wildlife Area
121 Newton Lake Fish and Wildlife Area
122 Oakwood Bottoms Federal Land
123 Red Hills State Park
124 Rend Lake State Park
125 Saline County Fish and
Wildlife Area
126 Stephen A. Forbes Fish and
Wildlife Area
127 Ten Mile Creek Fish and
Wildlife Area
128 Ten Mile Creek State Fish and
Wildlife Area: Eads Unit
129 Union County Wildlife
Management Area
130 Wayne Fitzgerrell State Park
131 White Squirrels of Olney and
Bird Haven

Suggested Reading

General Information

Admiraal, A.N., M.J. Morris, T.C. Brooks, J.W. Olson, and M.V. Miller. 1997. Illinois wetland restoration and creation guide. Illinois Natural History Survey Special Publication 19. viii + 188 pp.

Bellrose, F.C. 1980. Ducks, geese and swans of North America. Stackpole Books, Harrisburg, PA. 540 pp.

Bellrose, F.C. 1984. One state's contribution. Pages 342–346 in A.S. Hawkins, R.C. Hanson, H.K. Nelson, and H.M. Reeves, eds. Flyways: pioneering waterfowl management in North America. U.S. Department of Interior, Fish and Wildlife Service, Washington, DC.

Bellrose, F.C., and D.J. Holm. 1994. The ecology and management of the Wood Duck. Stackpole Books, Harrisburg, PA. 588 pp.

Bellrose, F.C., F.L. Paveglio, Jr., and D.W. Steffeck. 1979. Waterfowl populations and the changing environment of the Illinois River valley. Illinois Natural History Survey Bulletin 32:1–54.

Bohlen, H.D. 1989. The birds of Illinois. Indiana University Press, Bloomington. 221 pp.

Connett, E.V., ed. 1949. Wildfowling in the Mississippi Flyway. D. Van Nostrand Co., New York, NY. 387 pp.

Dahl, T.E. 1990. Wetlands: losses in the United States, 1780s to 1980s. U.S. Department of Interior, Fish and Wildlife Service, Washington, DC. 21 pp.

Day, A.M. 1959. North American waterfowl. Stackpole Books, Harrisburg, PA. 363 pp.

Fredrickson, L.H., and T.S. Taylor. 1982. Management of seasonally flooded impoundments for wildlife. Resource Publication 148. U.S. Fish and Wildlife Service, Fort Collins, CO. 29 pp.

Hanson, H.C. 1997. The Giant Canada Goose. Southern Illinois University Press, Carbondale. Rev. ed. 252 pp.

Havera, S.P. 1999. Waterfowl of Illinois: status and management. Illinois Natural History Survey Special Publication 21. xliii + 628 pp.

Hawkins, A.S., R.C. Hanson, H.K. Nelson, and H.M. Reeves, eds. 1984. Flyways: pioneering waterfowl management in North America. U.S. Fish and Wildlife Service, Washington, DC. 515 pp.

Illinois Department of Conservation. 1994. Aquatic plants: their identification and management. Fishery Bulletin No. 4, Illinois Department of Conservation, Springfield. 56 pp.

Illinois Department of Natural Resources. 1997. Digest of hunting and trapping regulations 1997–98. Illinois Department of Natural Resources, Springfield. 32 pp.

Johnsgard, P.A. 1975. Waterfowl of North America. Indiana University Press, Bloomington. 575 pp.

Linduska, J.P., ed. 1964. Waterfowl tomorrow. U.S. Fish and Wildlife Service, Washington, DC. 770 pp.

Madson, J. 1985. Up on the river. Nick Lyons Books, New York, NY. 276 pp.

Mills, H.B., W.C. Starrett, and F.C. Bellrose. 1966. Man's effect on the fish and wildlife of the Illinois River. Illinois Natural History Survey Biological Notes 57. 24 pp.

Mohlenbrock, R. 1988. A field guide to the wetlands of Illinois. Illinois Department of Conservation, Springfield. 244 pp.

Ratti, J.T., L.D. Flake, and W.A. Wentz. 1982. Waterfowl ecology and management: selected readings. The Wildlife Society, Bethesda, MD. 1,328 pp.

Suloway, L., and M. Hubbell. 1994. Wetland resources of Illinois: an analysis and atlas. Illinois Natural History Survey Special Publication 15. 88 pp.

Tiner, R.W., Jr. 1984. Wetlands of the United States: current status and recent trends. National Wetlands Inventory, U.S. Fish and Wildlife Service, Washington, DC. 59 pp.

Wesley, D.E., and W.G. Leitch, eds. 1987. Fireside waterfowler: fundamentals of duck and goose ecology. Stackpole Books, Harrisburg, PA. 346 pp.

Willms, P. and C. Wieda. 1996. Illinois public hunting areas report. Illinois Department of Natural Resources, Springfield. 25 pp.

Decoys and Calls

Christensen, R.D. 1993. Duck calls of Illinois, 1863–1963. Northern Illinois University Press, DeKalb. 275 pp.

Lacy, T. 1989. The wooden bird. Sun Foundation, Washburn, IL. 67 pp.

Parmalee, P.W., and F.D. Loomis. 1969. Decoys and decoy carvers of Illinois. Northern Illinois University Press, DeKalb. 506 pp.

Waterfowl Observation and Identification

Bull, J., and J. Farrand, Jr. 1986. The Audubon Society field guide to North American birds: eastern region. Alfred A. Knopf, New York, NY. 784 pp.

Carney, S.M. 1992. Species, age, and sex identification of ducks using wing plumage. U.S. Fish and Wildlife Service, Washington, DC. 144 pp.

DeLorme Mapping. 1991. Illinois atlas and gazetteer. DeLorme Mapping, Freeport, ME. 96 pp.

Farrand, J., Jr. 1983. The Audubon Society master guide to birding. Vol. 1. Loons to sandpipers. Vol. 2. Gulls to dippers. Vol. 3. Old world warblers to sparrows. Alfred A. Knopf, New York, NY.

LeMaster, R. n.d. The LeMaster method: waterfowl identification. Scotch Game Call Co., Elba, NY. 74 pp.

Madge, S., and H. Burn. 1988. Waterfowl: an identification guide to the ducks, geese and swans of the world. Houghton Mifflin Co., Boston, MA. 298 pp.

Murphy, M.K.J., and J.W. Mellen. 1997. Illinois wildlife and nature viewing guide. Illinois Department of Natural Resources, Springfield. 142 pp.

Robbins, C.S., B. Bruun, and H.S. Zim. 1983. Birds of North America: a guide to field identification. Western Publishing Co., Racine, WI. 360 pp.

Scott, S.L., ed. 1987. Field guide to the birds of North America. National Geographic Society, Washington, DC. 464 pp.

Food Habits

Anderson, H.G. 1959. Food habits of migratory ducks in Illinois. Illinois Natural History Survey Bulletin 27(4):289–343.

Bellrose, F.C. 1941. Duck food plants of the Illinois River valley. Illinois Natural History Survey Bulletin 21(8):237–280.

Bellrose, F.C., and H.G. Anderson. 1943. Preferential rating of duck food plants. Illinois Natural History Survey Bulletin 22(5):417–433.

Havera, S.P. 1999. Waterfowl of Illinois: status and management. Illinois Natural History Survey Special Publication 21. xliii + 628 pp.

Winterringer, G.S., and A.C. Lopinot. 1977. Aquatic plants of Illinois. Department of Registration and Education, Illinois State Museum Division and Department of Conservation, Division of Fisheries, Springfield, IL. 142 pp.

Nesting Structures

Ball, I.J., Jr. 1990. Artificial nest structures for Canada Geese. Fish and Wildlife Leaflet 13.2.12. U.S. Fish and Wildlife Service, Washington, DC. 8 pp.

Bellrose, F.C., and R. Crompton. 1983. Nest houses for Wood Ducks. Illinois Department of Conservation and Illinois Natural History Survey. 4 pp.

Vocalization

The following audio guides (CD or cassette) are available from Cornell Laboratory of Ornithology, 159 Sapsucker Woods Road, Ithaca, NY 14850:

Peterson Field Guide to Birdsongs of Eastern and Central North America

Peterson Field Guides to Western Bird Songs

National Geographic Society Guide to Bird Sounds

Bellrose, F.C. 1980. Ducks, geese and swans of North America. Stackpole Books, Harrisburg, PA. 540 pp.

Bull, J., and J. Farrand, Jr. 1986. The Audubon Society field guide to North American birds: eastern region. Alfred A. Knopf, New York, NY. 784 pp.

Farrand, J., Jr., ed. 1983. The Audubon Society master guide to birding. Vol. 1. Loons to sandpipers. Vol. 2. Gulls to dippers. Vol. 3. Old world warblers to sparrows. Alfred A. Knopf, New York, NY.

Robbins, C.S., B. Bruun, and H.S. Zim. 1983. Birds of North America: a guide to field identification. Western Publishing Co., Racine, WI. 360 pp.

MAX SCHNORF

Sunrise on the Mississippi River.

Internet Information

Illinois Department of Natural Resources
http://dnr.state.il.us/

Illinois Natural History Survey
http://www.inhs.uiuc.edu/

U.S. Fish and Wildlife Service
http://www.fws.gov/